The POWER of HABIT

Harnessing the Power to Establish Routines that Guarantee Success in Business and in Life

By

Jack D. Hodge

D0111987

This book is a work of non-fiction. Names and places have been changed to protect the privacy of all individuals. The events and situations are true.

ISBN: 1-4107-7996-3 (e-book)
ISBN: 1-4107-7995-5 (Paperback)

Library of Congress Control Number: 2003095700

This book is printed on acid free paper.

Printed in the United States of America
Bloomington, IN

1stBooks – rev. 09/10/03

DEDICATION

To my family – Amy, Hayden, Hunter, Holden

ACKNOWLEDGMENTS

This book is the result of a team effort. My deep thanks to those who have helped make it a reality:

First, I thank my wife Amy. For your unconditional love and your unwavering commitment to me and our boys, I cannot adequately describe my appreciation. Thanks also to Karen Admirral, Jimmy "I love Sushi" Isbell, The Trumbull Circle Gang, Doug E Fresh and the Cammster, and all my AZ buddies.

Finally, and certainly most important of all, I give all thanks to God the father, the Son, and the Holy Spirit for all that I am.

TABLE OF CONTENTS

INTRODUCTION

Success −1. The achievement of something desired, planned, or attempted: *attributed their success in business to hard work.* 2.a. The gaining of fame or prosperity: *an artist spoiled by success.* b. The extent of such gain. 3. One that is successful: *The plan was a success.*

-The American Heritage Dictionary

"In truth, the only difference between those who have failed and those who have succeeded lies in the difference of their habits. Good habits are the key to all success. Bad habits are the unlocked door to failure. Thus, the first law I will obey, which precedes all others, is −I will form good habits and become their slave."
-Og Mandino (The Greatest Salesman in the World)

Success is relative. Success is also subjective. We all have our own definition of what success means to us, and all of us have reached that definition of success to varying degrees. While most people wouldn't consider themselves failures, they probably would consider themselves less successful than they could be or would like to be. Whatever your definition of success, and however closely your life fits that definition, you probably have a pretty good idea of what it takes to be successful. If you're in a position of leadership you already know that clearly communicating a vision, clearly setting expectations, being a person of strong character, developing an atmosphere of trust, and leading by example are just a few of the many characteristics required to be a strong leader. If you're a salesperson you're already aware that knowing your products, knowing your competitor's products, knowing the market, knowing your customers, having great selling skills, and having a strong work ethic are just a few of the many characteristics required to be a highly successful salesperson. If your goal is to lead a healthier lifestyle, you already know the benefits of regular exercise and healthy eating habits. You already know that success will require you to maintain a consistent exercise program and reduce your intake of foods with a high fat content. The point is that you know what success looks like to you, and you probably already know what's required to achieve it.

The trick isn't in knowing *what's required* to make you more successful. The trick is in knowing *how to consistently do* the things that are required to make you more successful. Think about all the self-help books, videos, seminars, and television programs. The vast majority of people who read the books, watch the videos and TV programs, and go through the seminars fall short of any real change in their lives. Why? The reason is the self-help programs all focus on *what's required* to be successful –something we already know. Few, if any, explore *how to consistently do what's required* to be successful. This is ultimately what differentiates highly successful people from everyone else.

People who reach their ideal of success in life or in any particular endeavor consistently do things that make them more successful. How do they do it? Either consciously or subconsciously, the most successful people know how to establish habits and routines that guarantee their success. In fact, all highly successful people have one commonality – a routine based on good habits.

Habits are that important. Up to 90 percent of our everyday behavior is based on habit. Nearly all of what we do each day, every day, is simply habit. We all have good habits and bad habits, but if nearly 90 percent of what we do each day is habit, the only way to effect real change in our lives is to effect real change in our habits. The good news is that we can learn to effectively change bad habits and establish good habits that will make us more successful. The key to habit change is what this book delivers. It explains why the difference between those who are successful and everyone else is not found in differences in intelligence, talent, or work ethic; but rather in habits. It explores why habits are so powerful and how we can harness this power to reach our God-given potential and obtain a higher degree of success. The techniques outlined in this book will empower those who read it to transform their lives and become more successful.

Part One

Habits
and
Routines

Dreamers and Doers

At the end of the first semester of my freshman year of college, I was on the verge of flunking out of school. I skipped classes. I didn't keep up with the reading. I put off doing papers until it was too late. I tried, but I just couldn't seem to get my act together. That's when my grandfather sat me down to give me some grandfatherly advice; what he told me literally changed my life.

My grandfather explained to me, speaking as if his words were scientifically proven, time tested, matters of fact, that all people could be placed in one of two categories: Dreamers or Doers.

Jack D. Hodge

"There are only two kinds of people in this world: dreamers and doers," he explained. *"Dreamers talk about, think about, dream about, hope for, even plan on doing extraordinary things; doers do them!* Right now you're a dreamer, and it probably seems like no matter how hard you try you just can't get yourself to do the things that you know you should do or that you would like to do, but you can become a doer."

The advice given to me that day by my grandfather forever changed my life, and it can change yours too. So, if you're a dreamer how do you become a doer? What exactly is this transformation and how does it take place? Let's first take a closer look at what exactly a dreamer is and what constitutes a doer, and examine how the two differ.

Doers are more successful than dreamers because they take consistent, purposeful action, while dreamers never get started or quickly burn out. Doers have the ability to purposefully effect change in their lives. They accomplish extraordinary things, whether it's starting their own company, writing a book, getting elected to public office, running a marathon, or any other extraordinary accomplishment, while dreamers are somehow stuck on the sidelines only dreaming about doing such things.

What holds the dreamers back? Is it simply a fear of getting started? Is it fear of failure? Are the dreamers less talented, less intelligent? Is it a lack of ability or a lack of luck? What empowers the doer to do, to achieve and accomplish great things, while the dreamer is doomed to failure? The answer is simple, yet profound.

4

The force that empowers the doer yet holds back the dreamer is one and the same. It is HABIT.

Who Am I?

I am your constant companion. I am your greatest helper or heaviest burden. I will push you onward or drag you down to failure. I am completely at your command. Half the things you do you might just as well turn over to me and I will be able to do them quickly and correctly.

I am easily managed – you must merely be firm with me. Show me exactly how you want something done and after a few lessons I will do it automatically. I am the servant of all great individuals and, alas, of all failures as well. Those who are great, I have made great. Those who are failures, I have made failures.

I am not a machine, though I work with all the precision of a machine plus the intelligence of a human. You may run me for a profit or run me for ruin – it makes no difference to me.

Take me, train me, be firm with me and I
will place the world at your feet. Be easy
with me and I will destroy you.

Who am I?

I am HABIT.

2

The Power of Habit

Habit −1.a. A recurrent, often unconscious pattern of behavior that is acquired through frequent repetition.   b. An established disposition of the mind or character.   2. Customary manner or practice.

-The American Heritage Dictionary

"Nothing is more powerful than habit."

-Ovid

There is little question that we are creatures of habit. Like it or not, the habits we posses wield tremendous influence over our lives. Few people realize just how much influence.

It's said that up to 90 percent of our normal behavior is based on habit. Think about it. Most of our daily activities are simply habit. When and how we get up in the morning, shower, brush our teeth, dress, read the paper, eat, drive to work…hundreds of habits everyday. But habits go much deeper than just our daily routines. *Habits affect, if not control, every aspect of our lives.* From minute examples like biting your fingernails, twirling your hair, how you hold a pencil, and how you cross your arms, to more significant examples like your health –what you eat, how much you eat, when you eat, if you exercise, what type of exercise, how long, and how often. Even how we interact with friends, family and co-workers is all based on habits. In fact even a person's character is attributed to habit. Rick Warren, in his book *The Purpose Driven Life*, explains: "Your character is essentially the sum of your habits; it is how you habitually act." This notion that people's habits dictate their character is not new. Aristotle, around 350 B.C., proclaimed: "It is the habit of just and temperate actions that produces virtue." But the impact of our habits affect much more than just our individual lives. Many psychologists believe that habits actually guide psychological mechanisms of the entire social structure. Nineteenth-century psychologist William James wrote:

Habit is the enormous fly-wheel of society...It alone prevents the hardest and most repulsive walks of life from being deserted by those brought up to tread therein. It dooms us all to fight out the battle of life upon the lines of our nurture or our early choice, and to make the best of a pursuit that disagrees, because there is no other for which we are fitted, and it is too late to begin again. It keeps different social strata from mixing. Already at the age of twenty-five you see the professional mannerism settling down on the young commercial traveler, on the young doctor, on the young minister, on the young counselor-at-law. You see the little lines of prejudices, the ways of the "shop" in a word, from which the man can by-and-by no more escape than his coat-sleeve can suddenly fall into a new set of folds. On the whole, it is best he should not escape. It is well for the world that in most of us the character has set like plaster, and will never soften again.

James not only notes how the power of habit actually affects the entire social structure of society but he also points out how extremely difficult habits are to change.

"It is notorious how powerful is the force of habit."

-Charles Darwin

"It is generally felt to be a far easier thing to reform the constitution in Church and State than to reform the least of our own bad habits."

-Samuel Smiles

Why are habits so difficult to change? Because they are imbedded deep within our subconscious. This is why habits are nearly impossible to change using only our conscious will. Conscious effort works only while it's on guard, and can only overrule the subconscious when it is awake and alert. It's like a watch guard on duty. Late into the night the guard drifts off to sleep. That's when the subconscious takes over, because the subconscious never sleeps. The subconscious is always there, ready and waiting for the conscious watch guard to slip.

Have you ever set out to go somewhere in the car, and ended up somewhere else entirely before you realized you weren't going the right way? I drive the same route to work every day. Just recently crews began road construction along part of my route. Because the traffic is so bad due to the construction, I consciously planned out an alternate route to work. Unfortunately driving to work the same way for so long has become a habit. This habit is how my subconscious gets me to work. It's my autopilot of sorts. In the rush of the morning my conscious thoughts are preoccupied with numerous tasks, deadlines, and ideas, so my autopilot (subconscious) takes over and drives me to work. It's actually quite convenient, and allows me to do more with less effort. That is, until I need to change my subconscious (habit). Although I am consciously aware that traffic will be horrendous and make me late if I take my traditional route to work, my subconscious is not. The problem is, as my thoughts drift from avoiding traffic to pressing issues of the day, my subconscious takes over my driving, so of course I take the traditional route and end up stuck in traffic. *Therein lies the key to changing habits. Getting your conscious to communicate with, train, and reprogram your subconscious.*

Psychology 101

"*Nothing will happen to change your life until you consciously step in and start to work with your subconscious mind, otherwise, you will continue in the same pattern you have built up.*"

–Mildred Mann

Conscious vs. Subconscious

Think of your mind as consisting of two separate parts: the conscious and subconscious. Your conscious mind is your awareness. It thinks, reasons, calculates, plans, and sets goals. Your subconscious mind is a storage area of sorts. It's where your past experiences exist. Your memory, feelings, beliefs, values, and yes, your habits, all make up your subconscious.

You've probably heard that it takes 21 days to change a habit. There is some truth to this widely held belief and even some scientific data that backs it up. But 21 days is not a magic number. Different kinds of habits take different lengths of time to change. *The earlier a habit is formed in life (especially during early childhood), and the longer a habit exists (the more it's repeated), the more difficult the habit is to change.* My journey to work every morning, for example, did not take 21 days to change. It took about six days of me driving into the road construction and getting stuck in traffic before *my conscious got the attention of my subconscious and started training and reprogramming it.* On the other hand, I used to have the bad habit of biting my fingernails. This habit started in early childhood and lasted into my twenties. I owned that habit for a very long time, and it took me nearly 5 months to change it, well past the magic 21 days.

The following story further illustrates this point. One day a wise old teacher was taking a stroll through a forest with a young pupil at his side. The teacher suddenly stopped and took the time to point out four plants that were close at hand. The first plant was a tiny sprout, just coming out of the earth. The second plant was a more established sapling that had rooted itself firmly in the fertile soil. The third plant had grown into a well-developed tree standing nearly as high as the young pupil. The fourth plant was a mighty oak tree; the boy could scarcely see the top.

At this point, the teacher said to his youthful companion, "Pull up the first plant." The youngster pulled it up quite easily with his fingers.

"Now, pull up the second."

The young lad obeyed and with slight effort the plant came up, roots and all.

"And now, the third."

The young lad pulled with one hand and then with both. With great effort the young pupil strained. Finally the plant yielded to all his strength.

"And now, "said the wise old teacher, "try the fourth."

The young lad looked up at the enormous tree, and knowing firsthand the great struggle of pulling up a much smaller tree, he declined to even try.

"My son," the teacher exclaimed, "you have just demonstrated the power that habits will have over your life!"

The plants in the story represent habits. The older they get, the bigger they get, the deeper the roots grow, and the harder they are to uproot. Indeed, the fourth plant in the story was so massive, and represented such a daunting habit to change that the young pupil failed to even attempt to uproot it. The point is that some habits are more difficult to change than others. The good news is that this holds true not only for bad habits, but for good habits as well. When we create new good habits they are like the plants in the story. They grow from the sprout to the massive oak tree the more we repeat them and the longer we have them. Once we establish good habits they're as automatic as any other, and as difficult to change.

Habit vs. Addiction

It's important to note that there is a difference between a habit and an addiction. In a typical thesaurus habit is synonymous with inclination, tendency, and routine, whereas addiction is synonymous with fixation, chemical dependency, and obsession. This is an important distinction. Often habits and addictions exist together, but it's critical to separate the two. For example, when trying to change the habit of smoking it's helpful to realize that there is and an addiction involved. The addiction is the al dependency to the nicotine, the rest is the habit. le who smoke will have varying degrees of habit and addiction, but both habit and addiction are involved and they will both have to be dealt with in order to successfully stop smoking. This book deals strictly with habit and routine and does not attempt to address addiction.

3

The Benefits of Habit

"If you want to distance yourself from the masses and enjoy a unique lifestyle, understand this – your habits will determine your future."

-Jack Canfield

The Common Denominator

The one common denominator of all successful people is a routine built on good habits. The most successful people in any field –the most successful athletes, lawyers, politicians, physicians, business leaders, musicians, and sales people, *those who are the best at what they do have one thing in common: good habits.* This is not to say that they don't have bad habits, but they probably don't have many. A routine built on good habits is the distinguishing difference that separates the most successful people from everyone else. Their good habits enable them to more closely reach their genetic potential.

Think about it. Successful people are not necessarily more intelligent than anyone else, but their habits allow them to become more educated, more knowledgeable, and more competent. Successful people aren't necessarily more talented than average, but their habits allow them to become better trained, more practiced, and better prepared. Successful people aren't necessarily more determined or hard working than those who are less successful, but their good habits increase their resolve and commitment, and make them more efficient and organized.

It's not intelligence

You can thank your parents for your level of intelligence. Intelligence is genetic, and you can't change or increase your intelligence any more than you can change your height. But you can become more educated and more knowledgeable with the help of good habits. *Your habits determine how close you'll come to reaching your genetic potential.*

Let's say Dr. Jones, a family pr
develops the habit of reading medical
clinical studies every morning while she eats breakfast. Obviously, it won't take long for this habit to result in Dr. Jones becoming more educated, more knowledgeable, and indeed a more competent physician. To the outside observer it may appear that Dr. Jones is simply more intelligent than other physicians. The reality is that Dr. Jones is more intelligent than some doctors and less intelligent than others. But she can become more competent, and therefore seem more intelligent, than other physicians simply as a result of her habits.

Thomas Edison, arguably the greatest inventor of all time, created 1,093 inventions during his life including the light bulb, recorded music, and motion pictures. He was truly a genius. However, Edison himself credited his genius to his ability to develop his mind through the habit of thinking. Thomas Edison describes how this can be done: "The brain can be developed just the same as the muscles can be developed...it can be strengthened by proper exercise and proper use. By developing your thinking powers you expand the capacity of your brain and attain new abilities." He goes on to explain, "The man who doesn't make up his mind to cultivate the habit of thinking misses the greatest pleasure in life. He not only misses the greatest pleasure, but he cannot make the most of himself." Mr. Edison understood that the habit of thinking allows you to come closer to reaching your genetic potential.

Sarasate, the greatest Spanish violinist of the nineteenth century, was once called a genius by a famous critic. Sarasate sharply replied, "Genius! For thirty-seven years I've practiced fourteen hours a day, and now they call me a genius." Clearly Sarasate understood that it was not his genius or talent that made him the greatest violinist of his time, it was his habit of daily persistent practice that made the difference.

It's not talent or ability

Clearly Thomas Edison was a genius and an extremely talented inventor. However, he credited his success not to genius or talent, but to persistence and resolve. He once said, "Many of life's failures are people who did not realize how close they were to success when they gave up." Edison certainly was not in the habit of giving up. As talented as he was, it was his persistence and resolve that gave us the incandescent light bulb. It took him 10,000 tries before he found the right materials for his invention. The next time you flip on a light bulb, thank Thomas Edison's habit of never giving up, his relentless pursuit rather than his talent, for this incredible invention.

The habit of persistence also gave the game of basketball one of its greatest players. Larry Bird is a basketball legend. It's often said that he's one of the greatest players ever to play the game. There is no question that Bird was an unbelievable basketball player. There's also no question that he wasn't the most athletically gifted player. In fact, he wasn't even the most athletically gifted player on his team. In spite of his limited athletic ability, however, he led the

Boston Celtics to three world championships and remains one of the greatest players of all time. With limited talent, how could this happen? The answer, as you've probably guessed, is habit. Here is an example: Bird was one of the greatest free-throw shooters in NBA history. He grew up with the habit of practicing five hundred free-throw shots every morning before he went to school. With that habit, no matter what a person's innate talent or ability, they will become a fantastic free-throw shooter. Larry Bird is an excellent example of getting the most out of your God-given talents and abilities. Throughout his career, it was his disciplined habits that helped him reach his potential as an athlete.

So how important is talent and ability? Surely it must explain why the majority of the most successful people are so successful. Dr. Benjamin Bloom of the University of Chicago conducted a five-year study of leading scholars, artists, and athletes. The study consisted of anonymous interviews with the top twenty performers in their various fields, including pianists, tennis players, Olympic swimmers, sculptors, mathematicians, and neurologists. That information was supplemented by additional interviews with those individuals' families and teachers. Bloom and his research colleagues sought to find clues as to how these high achievers developed their skills and what common characteristics set them apart from those who are less successful. What they discovered was that the habit of persistence –continually striving to improve through practice in spite of setbacks and failures, and not talent or ability was responsible for their success.

It's not work ethic–
The difference really is habit

Have you ever known an "underachiever," somebody who is extremely intelligent or talented, yet just isn't as successful as they should be? In spite of their apparent potential, somehow they just can't seem to succeed to a level fitting their ability. Conversely, do you know an "overachiever," someone whose level of achievement or success exceeds their apparent abilities? They may not seem particularly intelligent or talented, yet somehow they succeed at whatever they do.

What's the difference between the underachiever and the overachiever? Often the underachiever is labeled as lazy, and the overachiever is labeled as hard working. But even laziness is really just the result of a multitude of bad habits – procrastination, disorganization, poor time management, lack of action, lack of commitment, lack of resolve. Similarly, a good work ethic is really just the culmination of good habits – organization, efficient time management, strong commitment, strong resolve, not procrastinating. The difference between the underachiever and the overachiever can be found by looking at the difference in their habits.

You may be thinking that work ethic is just a genetic trait. You may argue that we're either born with a good work ethic or we're not – that our work ethic is predetermined, inherited from our parents. If this is your thinking, you are partially correct; all traits are genetically inherited. But regardless of your genetic predisposition, your work ethic is greatly influenced by your environment. It's the old "nature vs. nurture" argument. We all have strong genetic tendencies (nature) which are heavily influenced by our upbringing, experiences, circumstances, and surroundings (nurture). How much is nature and how much is nurture will always be debated. It's clear, however, that our upbringing forges in us powerful habits that shape our work ethic.

The extent to which habits shape an individual's work ethic can be seen by examining the lives of identical twins. There are numerous stories of identical twins separated in early childhood and raised in different homes. One such story involves Bill and Jay, separated at age two. Jay grew up on a farm where every morning he woke up early to help with the chores. He also helped prepare meals, set the table, and helped clean up after dinner. When Jay had a rough first year playing Little League baseball, his father encouraged him to stick it out, explaining to Jay that he wasn't a quitter. Every day after school Jay practiced piano for 30 minutes and did his homework before he went out to play. Jay was raised to believe that hard work is honorable and gets a man far in life. His upbringing instilled in him a strong work ethic.

Jay's genetically identical twin brother, Bill, had a very different upbringing. He had little structure and was often left to take care of himself. Bill was not required to do chores and help around the house. No one talked about the importance of hard work and the benefits that result from always doing your best. Although as adults the two brothers share several uncanny commonalities, they have noticeably different work ethics. Again, the difference can be traced to their habits.

Good habits breed good consequences. Bad habits breed bad consequences

Imagine replacing your bad habits with desired good habits. Imagine how much more effective, efficient, and productive you would become.

We've established that the true hallmark of all successful people, the "doers" of the world, is action. Not just haphazard action, but consistent, purposeful action. We've also established that successful people aren't necessarily more intelligent, more articulate, more hardworking, or more determined. Successful people have developed good habits and established routines that make them more action-oriented and allow them to become more educated, communicate more effectively, and work more efficiently with more resolve. *In short, their habits and routines have allowed them to more closely reach their potential.* But how does developing good habits and routines translate into the consistent, purposeful action of the "doer"?

Take a personal inventory of all the bad habits you have. Now imagine replacing them with good habits you would like to have. For example, imagine:

- Always following up with commitments
- Never being late for meetings or appointments

- Never forgetting to return phone calls
- Communicating more effectively with colleagues, customers, family, etc.
- Always clearly setting expectations about expected outcomes and deadlines
- Quickly taking care of administrative work
- Actively listening
- Never waiting until the last minute to make plans and reservations
- Always remembering people's names after being introduced
- Maintaining good eye contact when talking with people
- Eating healthy everyday
- Exercising regularly
- Watching less TV
- Reading more
- Eating dinner together as a family every night
- Controlling your temper
- Investing and/or tithing at least ten percent of your income every month
- Regularly calling/writing friends and family members

Imagine the cumulative impact of these habits on your life.

Specific Habits and Broader Habits

The benefits of developing these specific habits translate into more significant, more far reaching benefits.

For example, let's say you develop three specific habits:

1. You quickly take care of administrative work instead of letting it pile up.
2. You quickly follow up with customers and colleagues.
3. You only handle items in your inbox once and complete them.

These three specific habits result in specific consequences:

1. Your administrative work is never late.
2. Customers and colleagues know they can count on you to follow up in a timely manner.
3. You begin to gain a reputation for getting things done quickly.

These specific consequences are somewhat obvious and predictable. But more significant consequences will soon become apparent. You start to procrastinate less in every area of your life. You become more organized. You become more efficient. As a result, you have more leisure time to do the things you want to do. This is nearly always the case when developing good habits. *Specific consequences of specific habits result in broader, more general habits with broader, more significant consequences.* These broader consequences are often more subtle and less predictable, yet they have a significantly greater impact on our lives.

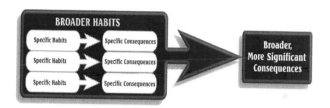

The benefits of changing bad habits and developing good habits are too numerous to even imagine. It's clear, however, that *your habits ultimately determine your level of success.* It's worth repeating: Good habits breed good consequences. Bad habits breed bad consequences.

The grass is always greener, so why not jump the fence?

"Many intelligent adults are restrained in thoughts, actions, and results. They never move further than the boundaries of their self-imposed limitation."

-John C. Maxwell

Are your habits holding you back? When I was a young boy I enjoyed spending time on my uncle's farm. There was no better place to run and play, but it wasn't all fun and games. I learned a lot about farming and about life. One lesson that has stuck with me started out as a morning walk through the pasture. As my uncle and I approached the electric fence, which was there to keep the cattle in, I wondered how we would get across. To my surprise, my uncle pushed down on the top wire and stepped over the fence to the other side. How had he not been electrocuted? As he motioned for me to follow his lead I hesitated. After all, this was the dreaded electric fence that I had so often been warned not to touch. Seeing my concern my uncle explained to me that electric fences don't need to be left on all the time. Once the cattle learn that they will be shocked, they will graze right up to the fence and stop. What really stuck with me was the fact that the grass on the other side of the fence was tall and lush, and must have looked quite appetizing to the cattle compared to the short, chewed, trampled grass they grazed on their side of the fence. But their past experiences had created habits that were holding them back.

"Our past is not our potential."
-Marilyn Ferguson

What self-imposed limitations have become habit in your life and are holding you back from reaching your full potential? Step over the powerless fences by changing bad habits and creating good habits. Don't let past experiences limit your future. Changing your habits is the key.

You are what you do daily

Routine –1. A prescribed, detailed course of action to be followed regularly; a standard procedure. 2. A set of customary and often mechanically performed procedures or activities.

-The American Heritage Dictionary

Jack D. Hodge

"You will never change your life until you change something you do daily. The secret of your success is found in your daily routine.

-John C. Maxwell

You are what you do daily. It's that simple. Whether you're getting better or worse, or staying the same, it all hinges on what you do from day to day. Your daily routine is that important. You may ask, What's the difference between habit and routine? The words are often used interchangeably. However, for our purposes we will define routine as the sum total and sequence of one's habits. In other words, all your habits throughout the day determine your daily routine. It's nearly impossible to overstate the importance of your daily routine in life. As stated earlier, the one common denominator of all successful people is a routine built on good habits. *The good news is that we all have the ability to choose our habits. We can purposefully change our habits and establish routines that will make us more successful.*

The Choice is yours
Living Life Intentionally

"We live our lives in chains and we never even know we have the key."

The Eagles – from the song "Already Gone"

Back to dreamers and doers. *Life doesn't just happen to the doer, the doer just happens to choose his life.* Doers live their lives intentionally instead of haphazardly. We all know that life thrusts itself upon us with unforeseen circumstances beyond our control. One of my favorite jokes is: "How do you make God laugh? Tell him your plans." We can't control everything that happens to us. In fact, the only thing we really can control is what we do daily. *We choose our actions throughout the day, every day, one day at a time. We choose our daily routines.* The problem is we too often choose not to choose. Remember, nearly 90 percent of what we do throughout the day is habit. Our actions are preprogrammed in our subconscious. Ninety percent of our choices have already been made and recorded in the program. We all have the power to change the program (our habits), but too often we don't realize that we have the power to choose, or we can't fathom the impact the choices have on our lives. The fact is, we can choose our habits and purposefully establish routines, and the consequences of our choices are enormous. Our conscious mind has the ability to train our subconscious mind. We therefore must decide to establish new routines consciously instead of forming more bad routines unconsciously. This is the essence of intentional living. Seize control of your habits, your daily routine, and your life. Take another look at the last line in the poem "Who am I" found in chapter 2:

Take me, train me, be firm with me and I will place the world at your feet. Be easy with me and I will destroy you.

Who am I?

I am HABIT

The Transformation
From Dreamer to Doer

"A single new habit can awaken within us a stranger totally unknown to us."

-Antoine de Saint-Exupery

"Do something you hate everyday, just for the practice."

-John C. Maxwell

The essential first step in transforming yourself from a dreamer to a doer is to: *"Do something you hate everyday, just for the practice."* This advice may not seem logical at first. In fact it may seem quite foolish or even masochistic. However, the first time I saw this quote I immediately appreciated the wisdom it held. Let me explain. I am an avid runner. I enjoy starting each day with an early, brisk 5K run. No matter how bad the weather is, heat, sleet, rain or snow, every morning I get at least a 5K run in. This hasn't always been the case however.

I used to hate getting up early. Mornings were always a struggle. I would have to drag myself out of bed with great effort. I cherished mornings I could sleep in. I frequently hit the snooze button three or four times before getting out of bed to face the day. I also hated running. I wasn't particularly good at it, and I found it difficult, boring, and downright painful. Getting up early every morning to run was the furthest thing from my mind. So how did I, the most unlikely runner, turn into the avid runner I am today?

The answer goes back to the advice my grandfather gave to me on the day that changed my life forever. He told me that in order to become a "doer," I needed self-discipline. He explained that no matter what I did, no matter how hard I tried, I could not reach my full potential until I mastered myself. This was the main tenet in his doctrine of "dreamers" and "doers" – self-mastery. This was the key. He explained how self-mastery could be achieved by following the advice found in his favorite quote from Mark Twain: *"Make it a point to do something every day that you don't want to do. This is the golden rule for acquiring the habit of doing your duty without pain."* My grandfather called this process *"practiced discipline,"* and went on to explain that if I did this every day without fail for one full month I would be well on my way to transforming myself into a doer. I followed the advice and chose running as my daily drudgery, my "practiced discipline."

Drudgery it was. I hated running, but I knew that it would be good for me. I was so out of shape I would literally get winded jogging to my mailbox and back, a distance of about 40 yards. I definitely needed some form of cardiovascular exercise, and I definitely hated running. So, running would be the one thing I did each day that I didn't want to do. My transformation started out slowly however. I dreaded getting up early, only to be rewarded with a painful run. I could only run a short distance before I was exhausted and out of breath. Practiced discipline did not seem to be working, and self-mastery did not look likely. But I kept in mind that I only had to force myself for one month. I did, and something strange began to happen.

As my physical condition slowly improved, the running got easier, which made dragging myself out of bed easier. By the end of one month the run was no longer drudgery. It was still difficult and took considerable effort, but it became tolerable. My daily ritual continued getting easier until I eventually looked forward to getting up to go for a run. I actually started to enjoy it. At this point, it took very little effort to wake up and go for a run each morning. It became a habit, a part of my routine. Now, I no longer have to coerce myself to run, I just do it.

This practiced discipline is essential for self-mastery, and self-mastery is essential for reaching your potential

> *"Self-command is not only itself a great virtue, but from it all the other virtues seem to derive their principle luster."*
>
> **Adam Smith**

> *"If you can win complete mastery over self, you will easily master all else. To triumph over self is the perfect victory."*
>
> **-Thomas Kempis**

> *"The greatest strength and wealth is self-control."*
>
> **-Pythagoras**

Self-mastery is vital. *You simply have no chance of changing your life and reaching your full potential without a high degree of self-mastery.* Sir Edmund Hillary of New Zealand, the first person to set foot on the top of Mount Everest, understood the importance of self-mastery. Avalanches, dehydration, hypothermia, and the physical and mental fatigue caused by the lack of oxygen at 29,000 feet all stood between him and the summit of the world's highest mountain. All those who dared to attempt the climb before Hillary had failed. He succeeded. When asked how he had conquered the mountain he explained: "It's not the mountain I conquered, but myself." Will power, self-mastery, self-control, self-discipline, whatever you choose to call it, you *can* develop it through practiced discipline by doing something you hate every day.

The benefits of self-mastery may at first appear obvious, but they are worth a closer look. Through my practiced discipline of daily running I increased my self-discipline, resolve, commitment, persistence, tenacity, efficiency, self-confidence, and self-esteem. The discipline also helped me develop the skill of setting goals and achieving them, and improved my ability to plan and execute. These are all essential skills needed to purposefully create habits and establish routines. Another example of just how important self-mastery is can be seen in the life of Teddy Roosevelt.

Teddy Roosevelt certainly understood the importance of self-mastery. In fact he often fancied himself as a "self-made man." Roosevelt is often regarded as the most physically fit, mentally tough leader this nation has ever had. But he didn't start out that way. As a child Roosevelt was afflicted with asthma so severe he was often too weak to blow out his bedside candle. Reflecting on his childhood, Roosevelt described himself as "a sickly, delicate boy" and "a wretched mite." His eyesight was poor, he was dangerously thin, and his condition was so grave that his parents weren't sure he would survive. But, survive he did.

Roosevelt explained: "Having been a rather sickly and awkward boy, I was a young man both nervous and distrustful of my own prowess. I had to train myself painfully and laboriously not merely as regards my body but as regards my soul and spirit." Roosevelt understood that he had to forge himself into the man he wanted to be through practiced discipline. In James M. Strock's book *Theodore Roosevelt on Leadership*, the author describes Roosevelt's struggle for self-mastery: "Rousing himself to achieve his potential, Teddy Roosevelt followed his father's guidance: 'You must make your body.'…One did not have the option of standing still; idleness left one vulnerable in the ongoing struggle for self-mastery." Journalist Henry Luther Stoddard recalled a conversation in which Roosevelt explained: "People talk much of my battles in life…The hardest battle I have had to fight, however, is one that no one knows about. It was a battle to control my self." Roosevelt went on to describe man's battle for self-mastery: "This he can get only by actual practice. He must, by custom and repeated exercise of self-mastery, get his nerves thoroughly under control. This is largely a matter of habit, in the sense of repeated effort and repeated exercise of will."

Evidence of Roosevelt's self-mastery can be seen throughout his life and in his daily routines. Even while president, he continued this practiced discipline. Looking back on his days in the White House, Roosevelt explained: "I always tried to get a couple of hours' exercise in the afternoons – sometimes tennis, more often riding, or else a rough cross-country walk." In a letter to a friend he described his day: "This morning I shook hands with six thousand people at the White House reception. This afternoon I took a two hours good hard ride with four of my children and a dozen of their cousins and friends; jumping fences, scrambling over wooded hills, galloping on the level." Roosevelt refused to waste time. If he wasn't engaged in some meaningful conversation, he was reading a book or writing a letter to a friend. Roosevelt was a man of action and was inclined to participate rather than be a mere spectator. Declining an invitation to attend a baseball game, he explained: "I will not sit for two hours and a half, and watch someone else do something." Roosevelt was often described by friends and foes as resolute, tenacious, and strongly committed to whatever task was at hand. All these characteristics resulted from his self-mastery.

Many of Roosevelt's friends and colleagues recognized Roosevelt's self-mastery. One of Roosevelt's boxing partners described Roosevelt as a "manufactured" rather than natural athlete. Historian Elting Morison observed: "There is apparent throughout his life a surprising determination. The energies and talents he possessed were not placed at birth in some natural harmony; they were through the passing years organized and directed by a sustained and splendid act of will."

It's important to remember that Roosevelt did not start out as a resolute, tenacious, physically fit, and mentally tough individual. Through the benefits of self-mastery he became this way. So what were Theodore Roosevelt's accomplishments? What type of man did he forge himself into? What were the results of his self-mastery?

- 26th president of the United States
- The youngest president in U.S. history
- The youngest vice president in U.S. history
- Held numerous public offices
- Asst. secretary of the navy
- Rough rider in the Spanish-American War
- Won the Medal of Honor
- Won the Nobel Peace Prize
- A great diplomat credited for ending several conflicts through negotiations and peace treaties
- Instrumental in the building of the Panama Canal
- Holds the Guinness world record for hand shaking (8,150 nonstop).
- Rode horseback 100 miles to demonstrate the level of fitness the military could and should achieve.
- After being shot in the chest while campaigning, went on to give 90-minute speech before going to the hospital.
- Defined the modern-day presidency (broke up monopolies, wielded the big stick, created the bully pulpit).
- President of the American Historical Assoc.
- Author of more than 30 books
- Founder of the NCAA
- Established the National Park system
- Established the National Forest Service
- Established the first federal game preserves

- o Established the first federal bird reserves
- o Established the first 18 national monuments, including the Grand Canyon

Not bad for a "timid and wretched soul," as he described himself. All these accomplishments, he admittedly reveals, were made possible in large part due to his high degree of self-mastery.

This transformation from dreamer to doer through self-mastery must take place in order to become as efficient, disciplined, resolute, resourceful and tenacious as we can be, in fact need to be, in order to reach our full potential. In essence, what self-mastery through practiced discipline will give you is the *ability* to purposefully create habits, not necessarily the *know-how*. Learning how to purposefully create habits and establish routines is the next step.

Choosing your daily drudgery – to each his own.

I chose daily running to help me develop a higher degree of self-mastery. Teddy Roosevelt chose a variety of physical activities and exercise. It doesn't matter what you choose, but it has to be something you have to force yourself to do. It also has to be something you can do daily. Finally, it should be something with beneficial side effects (e.g. exercise provides the benefits of physical fitness, increased energy, increased confidence, improved cognitive function, etc.).

Jack D. Hodge

Your daily drudgery can be any form of exercise such as running, weight training, swimming, biking, walking, aerobics, yoga, or martial arts. The choices of exercise are nearly endless. But it doesn't have to be exercise or physical activity. It can be practicing an instrument, educational reading or writing, correspondence through letters or e-mail, etc. The act itself is not important; the consistency of the act is. It's the self-discipline, the resolve, and the commitment that results from consistently doing something you hate every day that builds self-mastery.

Take the time now to think about and list some possibilities for your chosen daily drudgery:

1.) _____

2.) _____

3.) _____

4.) _____

5.) _____

Part Two

Habit
Change

Creating Habits /
Establishing Routines

Self-Examination
Who am I now? Who do I want to be?

Which habits are holding you back? Are you even aware of them? After the "transformation" described in chapter 5 takes hold, the first step in creating desired habits and establishing a productive routine is self-examination. *You must first identify the habits you wish to develop and the habits you wish to change. This step must involve people who work with us or are close to us who can help us identify bad habits that we are unaware of.* This may seem like common sense at first, and too obvious to mention, but it's an important step that definitely is worth mentioning.

> *"Nothing so needs reforming as other people's habits."*
>
> *-Mark Twain*

> *"Self-knowledge is the beginning of self-improvement."*
>
> *-Spanish proverb*

Many of the habits that hinder our success are obvious to us. Others are more difficult to identify. We are often unaware of the habits that hinder our success and hold us back. As Oliver Wendell Holmes points out, "We all need an education in the obvious." The following story illustrates this point:

When I was a boy the circus came to our small town in Southwest Indiana, and throngs of people gathered to watch the raising of the tent. My brother and I were fascinated by the incredible power of the elephants as they raised the massive tent beams and stretched the tent canvas into form.

That night, we attended the circus production under the big top. My brother and I immediately noticed the elephants standing quietly while tied to small wooden stakes. "Dad, why don't the elephants pull the stakes out of the ground and run away?" my brother asked. My father, a little surprised himself, asked one of the elephant handlers.

The elephant handler explained that while young and much less powerful, an elephant is tied by a heavy chain to an immovable steel stake. The young elephant tries day after day to escape the chain, but to no avail. The animal discovers that, no matter how hard he pulls, the chain will not break and the stake remains secure. The young elephant eventually gives up. At this point the elephant starts building a habit of not trying. This habit is repeated day after day until, as a grown elephant, he continues to believe that he cannot move as long as there is a stake in the ground beside him, no matter how small or insecurely fastened.

People can be "trained," or as psychologists put it, "conditioned" to behave like these elephants. They are restricted by old habits in thought, action, and results. Therefore, they're unknowingly trapped by their self-imposed limitations.

We can usually identify several bad habits that are holding us back, and good habits that will allow us to come closer to reaching our potential. But we can't identify all of them. *Often we have habits we aren't even aware of that are holding us back.* This is where self-awareness comes in.

Self-awareness is the overlap of how we think others perceive us and how others really do perceive us. The more self-awareness we have, the more accurate our perception of how others see us is.

We may think we are perceived one way when in fact we are commonly seen in a much different light.

Oswald Chambers describes this lack of self-awareness as a detrimental, pervasive conceitedness: "It is astounding how ignorant we are about ourselves...We have to get rid of the idea that we understand ourselves, it is the last conceit to go."

Consider Sally, for example. Sally is a senior sales manager for a large pharmaceutical company. She fancied herself as a highly competent, visionary leader with strong communication skills whom subordinates would freely come to for help. In reality her subordinates dreaded asking her for feedback or help. They perceived that she communicated poorly and would frequently take over their work to ensure that the job was done "right". They secretly complained that she reluctantly gave up responsibility and had difficulty empowering employees. Sally had a reputation of being a "control freak." Her employees also complained that they never received positive feedback even when their performance was superb. Many of her subordinates and peers complained, "We never know where we stand." Clearly, how others saw Sally was very different than how she saw herself.

It's not as if Sally didn't care how she was being perceived. But she incorrectly assumed that she could decipher this information herself. Worse, she believed that if she was having a negative effect, someone would tell her.

Sally was having a negative effect, and she would have continued not receiving feedback from her subordinates and not knowing how they really perceived her if not for an anonymous feedback program her company instituted. Through a program called "360° feedback" she discovered that she was

much less effective than she had thought. The 360°
feedback program solicits anonymous feedback from
coworkers. This allows employees to get an accurate
picture of how others perceive them, in order to help
them identify strengths and weaknesses. After
identifying several negative behaviors (bad habits) that
were holding her back, Sally could then begin to work
on changing them. Becoming aware of these habits
was the first step toward changing them.

There are several anonymous feedback surveys
available. 360° feedback is just one of many used by
corporations to help employees identify otherwise
unknown negative behaviors (bad habits) which
prevent people from reaching their potential. If you
work for a corporation it's worth checking to see
whether a feedback program like this is available. If
anonymous feedback surveys are not available to you,
there are a number of self-surveys that can help
pinpoint negative traits that may be holding you back.
The Herrmann Brain Dominance Profile, DiSC
program, and the Meyers Briggs Personality Inventory
are just a few of the many self-surveys that are
available. Another great way to get this information is
to seek it and encourage it from colleagues and family
members. It may be somewhat diluted when we
receive it, but if we make it a point to solicit feedback
from others we will start to get this much-needed
feedback, and as a result begin to improve our self-
awareness.

List of Web sites containing some popular self-survey systems:

Personality Profiles

www.prep-**profiles**.com/docs/samplereport.html

www.interviewwww.stehouwer.com/Selectyourtest.html

www.interviewtech.com/drakeipmsystemfaq.asp

www.**profiles**rus.com/

www.eliteweb.com/proteam/of.htm

www.competitiveedgeinc.com/Products.html

www.daltonalliances.com/assessment.asp

humanresources.about.com/cs/**personality**tests/

Anonymous Feedback

www.**360-degree**feedback.com/

www.allpointsfeedback.com/

www.panoramicfeedback.com/

www.halogensoftware.com/products/index.php

www.entegrys.com/

www.nefried.com/**360**/

www.3dgroup.net/page25.html

resourcesunlimited.com/**feedback**.asp

www.organizedchange.com/Excite/360degreefeedback.htm

www.craftsystems.com/csnew/**360**.htm

www.**feedback**360.net/

www.**ifeedbackonline.com**/360-degree-**surveys.htm**

Self – Examination Results

Take time now to list several bad habits and desired good habits:

Bad Habits

_____

_____

_____

_____

_____

_____

_____

_____

_____

Desired Good Habits

_____

_____

_____

_____

_____

_____

_____

_____

_____

Replace, Not Erase

"One habit overcomes another."

-Thomas Kempis

After identifying which habits you wish to develop and which habits you wish to change, it's important to understand how changing a habit works. It's often said that habits are hard to break. This is an inaccurate statement. *Habits aren't broken; they are replaced. In other words, you replace, not erase, bad habits.* This is an important distinction because if we are to change a bad habit we must carefully consider which habit we are to replace it with.

You may know a former smoker who after quitting the habit of smoking, without forethought, replaced that habit with the habit of eating. The result was overeating, and the former smoker put on weight. There are other theories as to why this frequently happens to people who quit smoking, but it's clear that when you quit a habit it creates a vacuum that must be filled with something. Therefore it's important to purposefully choose what that something will be to avoid replacing one bad habit with another.

I was reminded of the importance of choosing habits during a fishing trip I recently took in Canada. Even in July, the early morning air was chilly enough to require a coat. I was told that the area of Canada we were fishing experiences only two seasons –winter and July. When the backroads of that remote area thaw in the summer, they become muddy, and vehicles traveling through the backcountry leave deep ruts in the roads. The ground freezes hard in the winter months, and the deep frozen ruts become part of the traveling challenges. For vehicles entering this undeveloped area during the winter, there is a road sign that reads: "Drivers, please choose carefully which rut you drive in, because you'll be in it for the next 20 miles." Habits can be much like these ruts. They determine the direction of your life, whether you're headed for success or failure. And, once chosen, you are stuck with them for a long time. Therefore you must carefully choose the habits that make up your life.

It also makes it much *easier* to change a bad habit if you *purposefully* choose the new habit that will replace it. Take for example the habit of chewing tobacco. I have a friend who quit chewing tobacco using several habit-changing techniques, including replacing the habit of chewing tobacco with the habit of chewing sunflower seeds. Every time he got the urge to put in a "chew" he instead would chew on sunflower seeds. He's now reached the point where he no longer chews sunflower seeds either, but he will tell you that the sunflower seeds were needed for a long time.

Another friend of mine had the bad habit of watching TV while in bed at night until he fell asleep. He purposefully replaced that habit with the habit of reading each night in bed until he was sleepy enough to fall asleep. Again, *purposefully choosing new habits to replace old habits will greatly increase your chances of changing bad habits.*

Conversely, when purposefully creating and establishing a good habit, it helps to realize that you are replacing some other habit. For example, if you want to create the habit of doing sit-ups first thing every morning, you must realize that you already have the habit of doing something else first thing every morning. If you want to develop the habit of actively listening, then you must realize that you are in the habit of not actively listening. This is what you must *specifically* identify. The habit of not actively listening may mean that your thoughts are preoccupied with what you'll say next, and not with what's being said. You miss some of the message the person is trying to communicate because you are focused on your response. Or you could be in the habit of letting your mind wonder off the conversation onto thoughts of other things you must do that day. Knowing specifically what habit you are replacing will help you more readily recognize when you are engaged in the bad habit. This is key; it's very difficult to change a bad habit if you aren't aware of when you are doing it. *You greatly increase your chance of successfully creating a new habit if you specifically identify the habit you are replacing.*

Take time now to make a list of the habits you'd like to change and habits you'd like to replace them with (the more specific the better):

Bad habits to be change	Good habits to be developed
_____	_____
_____	_____
_____	_____
_____	_____
_____	_____
_____	_____
_____	_____
_____	_____
_____	_____
_____	_____

Consequences–
The "attention getters" of the subconscious

"Man cannot remake himself without self-imposed consequences, for he is both the marble and the sculptor."

-Dr. Alexis Carrel

Negative consequences

Consequences, both positive and negative, are the "attention getters" of the subconscious. Remember that habits lie deep within the subconscious. Also remember that in order to change a habit the conscious mind has to get the attention of, communicate with, train, and reprogram the subconscious. Therefore, there must be consequences when we repeat a bad habit or fail to reinforce building a good habit. It's very similar to training a pet. If when a puppy wets on the floor he receives a gentle swat, the puppy will begin to associate wetting on the floor with the discomfort of a swat.

Many parents know that one way to help children stop sucking their thumb is to put a bad-tasting substance on the child's thumb. The child starts to associate the negative consequence of the bitter taste with sucking his or her thumb.

I had the bad habit of biting my fingernails. I would often bite my fingernails and not even be aware I was doing it. To change this habit I instituted a negative consequence. When I (my conscious mind) would realize I was biting my fingernails, I would bite down on my little finger hard enough to cause discomfort (one of the "attention getters" of the subconscious). Soon, I became aware that I was biting my fingernails as soon as I started. Before long, I realized when I was about to start biting my fingernails before my fingers even reached my mouth. With the continued negative consequence, my conscious mind got the attention of my subconscious, and eventually I no longer had the habit of biting my fingernails.

When bad habits are repeatedly followed by consequences, you are in essence training your subconscious. Your subconscious eventually associates the bad habit, or failing to reinforce the desired good habit, with the negative consequences. Once this happens, you are well on your way to habit change.

It's important to realize that bad habits generally result in negative consequences regardless of any consequences you may purposefully add. Yet these natural consequences are obviously not enough to deter the recurrence of the bad habit. It's also important to note that many self-help programs suggest there should be no consequences for "failing" and slipping back into a bad habit or not following through with a resolution. They often put forth excuses such as "realize you're only human" or "no one is perfect" or "don't beat yourself up." This thinking is short-sighted and will jeopardize your chances of success. Instead, it's helpful to think of "failing" as "training." As such, we need to provide consequences for ourselves, both positive and negative.

Positive consequences

The other "attention-getter" of the subconscious is pleasure. Going back to our example of the puppy, if you want to train the puppy to sit, bark or shake on command, you use the positive reinforcement of giving the dog a treat and telling him he's a good boy while you pet him. The positive reinforcement (positive consequences) are the pleasure in eating the treat, the affirming tone of your voice, and the positive attention of you petting him. The puppy quickly associates the positive consequences with the desired trick.

Parents understand the power of positive consequences. Some friends of ours used positive consequences to help their children develop the habit of making their beds every morning. If the child made his bed his mother would make him a hot breakfast that morning. If the child didn't make his bed he was on his own with cold cereal. The children are now young men in college. They no longer receive the positive consequence of Mom's hot breakfast, but they still make their beds...every morning.

A colleague of mine used to have the annoying habit of finishing people's sentences and correcting their grammatical errors when they spoke. He confided in me that he changed these habits by using positive consequences. He loved pistachio nuts. Each time he started to finish someone's sentence or correct their grammar and successfully stopped himself, he would reward himself with a handful of pistachios. He soon became very good at catching himself before he spoke, and now he no longer has these annoying habits.

One reason this positive consequence technique may have been so successful with my coworker is because he kept a stash of pistachios in his desk drawer all day. He longed for those pistachios that were so close at hand. This kept the bad habit at the forefront of his thoughts. His conscious mind was therefore always on the lookout for opportunities to train his subconscious. Eventually his subconscious learned that his conscious would not allow him to partake in the pleasure of the pistachios unless he successfully stopped himself from cutting someone off and finishing their sentence or rudely correcting their grammar. *Getting your conscious mind to communicate with, train, and reprogram your subconscious is the key to habit change.*

Take time now to make a list of possible consequences (positive and negative) to reinforce a change in habit.

Positive Consequences

_____

_____

_____

_____

_____

_____

_____

_____

_____

Negative Consequences

_____

_____

_____

_____

_____

_____

_____

_____

_____

Mental Dress Rehearsal

"All acts performed in the world begin in the imagination."

-Barbara Grizzuti Harrison

Athletes have long realized the importance of mental rehearsal and visualization. You've probably witnessed long-jumpers visualizing their jumps by pantomiming the approach, jump, and landing before actually performing each jump. You've probably seen basketball players mentally rehearsing their free-throw shots by actually practicing the shot with no ball. You more than likely have seen field-goal kickers visualize kicking the ball through the goal-post. One of golf's greatest players, Jack Nicklaus, explained how he utilizes mental rehearsal techniques before each swing: "First I 'see' the ball where I want it to finish, nice and white and sitting up high on the bright green grass. Then the scene quickly changes, and I 'see' the ball going there: its path, trajectory, and shape, even its behavior on landing. Then there's a sort of fade-out, and the next scene shows me making the kind of swing that will turn the previous images into reality." Mentally practicing exactly how the athlete will perform the task and visualizing a successful outcome greatly increase the athlete's performance. Likewise, mentally rehearsing how we react in certain situations can greatly increase our ability to change undesirable, automatic behaviors (bad habits).

Let's say you identify that you have the bad habit of reacting poorly when confronted with bad news. Through feedback, you learn that when you receive bad news you are often seen as overreacting. Being aware of this bad habit and when it occurs is obviously the first step. The second step will be to identify which positive habit you want to replace the negative habit with (remember you replace, not erase, habits). Once the bad habit and the situations that set it off are identified, and you specifically identify how you will now react when confronted again with such a situation, the next step is mental preparation.

Mentally rehearsing how you will react in given situations is crucial to changing habits. Researchers at the University of Pittsburgh and Carnegie Mellon University have shown that as we prepare for a task by mentally rehearsing our desired behavior, we activate the prefrontal cortex – the part of the brain that moves us into action. The greater the mental preparation, the better we perform the task. In fact, brain studies have shown that mental preparation: imagining a behavior in vivid detail can activate the same brain cells actually involved in doing the activity. The researchers found that this mental preparation is particularly important when trying to replace a bad habit with a good habit. This is because the prefrontal cortex becomes particularly active when a person prepares to overcome a habitual response. The aroused prefrontal cortex focuses the brain on what's about to happen and how it will respond. Without this activation of the prefrontal cortex, the person will more than likely react in the ingrained, undesirable behavior.

Conversely, with mental practice and the resulting activation of the prefrontal cortex, we are much more likely to perform our rehearsed, desired response when faced again with such a situation. Take for example our friend Sally, the senior sales manager who was introduced at the beginning of the chapter. Through feedback Sally identified the specific bad habit of responding poorly to bad news. She decided to replace this bad habit with a new response. Sally envisioned herself being the "cool head of reason" when things were not going well. She envisioned herself speaking in an empathetic tone, thinking clearly with a level head, keeping things in perspective, and controlling her emotions. Sally then practiced her desired response over and over in vivid detail in her mind. Now, when confronted with bad news, her brain responds the way it has so many times in mental practice. She now is the "cool head of reason" that she desired to be in such situations.

Rome wasn't built in a day –
One step at a time. One habit at a time.

"A journey of a thousand miles must begin with a single step."

–Chinese proverb

"Sow an act, reap a habit; sow a habit, reap a character; sow a character, reap a destiny."

-G.D. Boardman

Trying to change more than one habit at a time is not a good idea. Attempting to do too much at once will likely result in failure. But you can effect significant change in your life by changing just a few habits. Remember that *specific consequences of specific habits result in broader, more general habits with broader, more significant consequences.* These broader, more significant consequences are often more subtle and less predictable, yet they have a much greater impact in our lives.

Recall the list of good habits from Chapter 3. Imagine:

- always following up with commitments
- never being late for meetings or appointments
- never forgetting to return phone calls
- communicating more effectively with colleagues, customers, and family
- always clearly setting expectations about expected outcomes, and deadlines
- quickly taking care of administrative work
- actively listening
- never waiting until the last minute to make plans and reservations
- always remembering people's names after being introduced
- making good eye contact when talking with people
- eating healthy everyday
- exercising regularly
- watching less TV

- reading more
- eating dinner together as a family every night
- controlling your temper
- investing or tithing ten percent of your income every month

There are 17 habits listed here. It's generally believed that it takes 21 days to change a habit. Although some habits take less time to change and many take more time to change, this is a good number to work with. If the average habit takes 21 days to change, then by changing one habit at a time, this list of 17 good habits could be yours in one year. That's significant change, one habit at a time.

The Power of Focus

We all know how difficult habits are to change, and we've established many reasons why this is so. In order to change habits, we have to get the attention of, communicate with, and train our subconscious. This is no easy task. That is why it's so important to attempt changing only one habit at a time. Changing habits requires the power of focus. To illustrate the power of focus consider the analogy of focusing light.

Diffused light has very little power, but you can concentrate the energy of light by focusing it. When rays of light from the sun pass through a magnifying glass, the light is focused and now has the power to set fire to paper or grass. When light is focused further, such as in the beam of light from a laser, it can cut through steel.

Such is the power of focus when it comes to changing our habits. Focusing our conscious effort on changing one habit at a time gives us incredible power to reprogram our subconscious. Attempting to change *more* than one habit diffuses our efforts and drastically decreases our abilities to change our habits.

The Power of Momentum and the Law of Inertia

Inertia – 1. The tendency of a body at rest to remain at rest or of a body in motion to remain in motion unless acted on by an outside force. 2. Resistance to motion, action, or change.

-The American Heritage Dictionary

"With enough momentum, nearly any kind of change is possible."

-John C. Maxwell

With each habit change, we get better at changing habits.

If you were to place a doorstop under the front wheel of a train, the train would be unable to move. Even with its massive engines going full bore the train would remain motionless. On the other hand, if a train is moving with a good head of steam it is nearly impossible to stop. How can this be? How could such a small object as a doorstop prevent something as massive and powerful as a train from moving? Why is it that once in motion the train is nearly impossible to stop? The answer is inertia. A train standing still has to overcome the inertia of its own massive weight. It takes an enormous amount of energy to move the entire weight of the train. Conversely, it takes an enormous amount of energy to stop the train's massive weight once it's in motion. And, the faster it's going, the more difficult it is to stop. This is referred to as momentum, and it can be an enormous ally to help us create habits.

When we first start out, trying to change habits is extremely difficult. We find that, much like a motionless train, it's hard for us to get started. But, after changing that first habit, it gets a little easier. In fact *with each habit change, we get better at changing habits.* We actually start to develop the habit of changing habits. When this happens we are like the unstoppable train in motion. Momentum is on our side and living intentionally starts to become a reality.

Think Big But Start Small
The power of incrementalism

"The man who moves a mountain begins by carrying away small stones."

–Chinese proverb

Not only is it best to focus on changing one habit at a time, but when deciding what to change, you also have to start small. If, for instance, you decide to run a marathon, but are not currently a runner, you obviously have to start out by running short distances. It can be done, however, using the principle of incrementalism. Incrementalism is the phenomenon of small, steady improvements over time resulting in immense change. There is great power in incrementalism. The non-runner who starts out by only running 400 yards can eventually run a full marathon. I'm living proof. But it requires developing the habit of consistently running, if only for a short distance. You start with 400 yards, then 600 yards, then a half-mile. Before long, your half-mile limit turns into your first 5k race, and so on, until finally it's race day for the Boston Marathon. I don't want to give the false impression that it's easy. Obviously for a non-runner to achieve such a goal would take developing a strong habit of consistent running as well as tremendous effort, but it can be done. Accomplishing any habit change is much easier and your chances for success are much greater when you start small and utilize the power of incrementalism.

My oldest son now understands the power of incrementalism. He has become a fairly talented piano player, and enjoys playing. I enjoy listening to him practice, but this was not always the case. At first playing the piano was a struggle for him. He did not enjoy practicing and gave my wife and me a great deal of grief for putting him through it. Because we had made a large investment in a new piano and prepaid lessons, we asked him to stick with it for a little longer.

In his first lesson he started out using just two keys. The lessons got more difficult and more complex over time as his abilities and understanding developed. Now it's a pleasure to listen to him play, and he actually enjoys playing. Slow, steady improvement was the key to my son's development as a pianist. Think about it: Even the world's greatest concert pianist started by using just a few keys at a time. In the same way, slow steady improvement is the key to developing any habit.

> *"One step and then another, and the longest walk is ended.*
> *One stitch and then another, and the longest rent is mended.*
> *One brick upon another, and the tallest wall is made.*
> *One flake and then another, and the deepest snow is laid."*
>
> *-Anon*

Boiling Frogs

The power of incrementalism can also work against us. It's said that if you were to place a frog in boiling water, the frog would immediately jump out. But if you were to place a frog in water and then slowly bring the water to a boil, the frog would remain in the water unaware of the gradual change until it was

71

too late. We are much like frogs in this respect. If changes are gradual enough they go unnoticed. We all have deeply ingrained bad habits, but they didn't just suddenly appear. We developed them over time, often unaware they were taking hold. This, again, is why living intentionally is so important. We can choose to change and develop good habits, but so often we choose not to choose and life just happens to us. Beware, you could be a frog in water that's rapidly coming to a boil.

The Power of Persistence

SYNONYMS: perseverance, persistence, tenacity, pertinacity. Each of these nouns means steadfast singleness of purpose, as in the pursuit of a goal, despite difficulties or obstacles. *Perseverance* suggests praiseworthy and enduring patience.
                              -The American Heritage Dictionary

"I do not think there is any other quality so essential to success of any kind as the quality of persistence. It overcomes almost everything, even nature."

John D. Rockefeller

There is one essential trait for any kind of change to take hold. In fact all prerequisites for successfully changing habits culminate in this one overriding quality – persistence. As mentioned earlier, self-mastery gives us the *ability* to change habits. In fact, our ability to change habits is directly proportional to our level of self-discipline. Our level of self-discipline is evidenced by our persistence. As Sir Winston Churchill once put it: "Persistence is self-discipline in action."

Famed psychologist and philosopher, William James, observed, "If an unusual necessity forces us onward, a surprising thing occurs. The fatigue gets worse up to a certain point, when, gradually or suddenly, it passes away and we are fresher than before!" James continues, "We have evidently tapped a new level of energy. There may be layer after layer of this experience, a third and fourth 'wind'. We find amounts of ease and power that we never dreamed ourselves to own, sources of strength habitually not taxed, because habitually we never push through the obstruction of fatigue."

If we have developed a high degree of self-discipline we will have the persistence required to push through what James describes as "the obstruction of fatigue" to ultimately reach our goals. James also points out that persistence is habitual. The extraordinary thing about the habit of persistence is that the more persistent we are, the more persistent we become. The fact is persistence is essential to changing our habits and reaching our goals.

> *"There are but two roads that lead to an important goal and to the doing of great things: strength and perseverance. Strength is the lot of but*

> *a few privileged men; but austere*
> *perseverance, harsh and continuous,*
> *may be employed by the smallest of us*
> *and rarely fails of its purpose, for its*
> *silent power grows irresistibly greater*
> *with time."*
>
> *-Johann von Goethe*

So, how are we to know when we have persevered enough? What amount of persistence is required? The answer is, when we have achieved what we set out to do –when we have reached our goal. We should anticipate and expect setbacks, but we should not mistake them for failure. We must realize that all successful people experience setbacks but do not accept them as defeat. Setbacks are merely the exhaust of active, doing people – the doers of the world.

Persistence in Action –
Famous Failures that Proceeded Success

- In his first years in the automobile business, Henry Ford went bankrupt twice.
- In 1902, the poetry editor of the *Atlantic Monthly* returned the poems of a twenty-eight-year-old poet with the following note: "Our magazine has no room for your vigorous verse." Robert Frost persevered.
- Inventor Chester Carlson pounded the streets for years before finding investors for his Xerox photocopying process.

- Michael Jordan was cut from his high school basketball team.
- Dr. Seuss' first children's book was rejected by twenty-three publishers. The twenty-fourth publisher sold over six million copies and Dr. Seuss died having known his perseverance resulted in entertaining, challenging, and educating millions of children.
- During its first year of business, the Coca-Cola company sold only 400 cokes.
- After having been rejected by both Atari and Hewlett-Packard, Apple computers netted first-year sales of over $2.5 million.
- Charles Goodyear was obsessed with the idea of making rubber that was unaffected by temperature extremes. Years and years of unsuccessful experimentation caused bitter disappointment, imprisonment for debt, family difficulties, and ridicule from friends. He persevered, and in February of 1839 discovered that adding sulfur to rubber achieved his purpose, leading to the first Goodyear tires.
- Marathoner Joan Benoit underwent knee surgery only seventeen days before the U.S. Olympic trials, but her persistence and determination enabled her not only to make the team, but also to win the first ever Olympic gold medal in her event.
- In 1905, the University of Bern rejected a Ph.D. dissertation, saying that it was

irrelevant and fanciful. Albert Einstein was disappointed but not defeated. He persevered.

* Frank Woolworth labored for years only to see his first three chain stores go bankrupt. He persisted until Woolworth's stores became a phenomenal success.

Johnny loved football and played quarterback for St. Justin High School in Pittsburgh. He attempted to make the Notre Dame football team but was judged too small. He settled for playing at a smaller college. Upon graduation, his bid to play for the Pittsburgh Steelers ended when he was cut from the team. Johnny worked in construction and played some amateur football while staying in contact with every NFL team. All he wanted was a chance. His persistence paid off. The Baltimore Colts responded, and he soon became the top quarterback in the league, leading the Colts to a world championship. Ultimately, Johnny Unitas was inducted into the Football Hall of Fame and is remembered as one of the greatest quarterbacks of all time.

While a student at Yale, Fred Smith came up with an innovative airfreight concept sure to revolutionize the way we send and receive packages. He submitted his idea as a term paper in his economics class. What was his grade for this ingenious new idea? His professor returned his paper with a big C written in red ink, and this note: "The concept is interesting and well-formed, but in order to earn better than a C, the idea must be feasible." In spite of this disappointing setback, Smith persisted and eventually raised $72 million in loans and equity investments. The company endured several more setbacks and disappointments, and suffered heavy losses during the first several years before finally realizing a profit of a mere $20,000 in 1975. But Smith's persistence finally did pay off. Today, Smith's visionary company operates in 210 countries, employs 140,000 people, and delivers 3 million packages per day. As the founder and CEO of Federal Express, Fred Smith's ability to persevere and relentlessly pursue his dream has created a $7 billion company based on an idea not considered "feasible."

Louis Pasteur is considered by many to be the greatest biologist of the nineteenth century. In fact, if one were to choose among the greatest benefactors of humanity, Louis Pasteur would certainly rank toward the top of the list. He is the founder of microbiology, and his work paved the way for branches of science and medicine such as stereochemistry, bacteriology, virology, immunology, and molecular biology. His discovery that most infectious diseases are caused by germs, known as the "germ theory of disease," is one of the most important discoveries in medical history. He saved the silk industry through his work on silkworm diseases, and he developed vaccines for anthrax, cholera, and rabies. Perhaps Pasteur is best known for his revolutionary discovery of a process for heat-treating foods to retard spoilage and prevent microbe-related food poising in humans. This process, still known today as pasteurization, has safeguarded our food supply for generations. What's less known is that Pasteur suffered several devastating strokes resulting in debilitating health problems, including paralysis of his entire left side. In spite of these physical limitations and several other personal tragedies, he persisted and continued his important work. "Let me tell you the secret that has led me to my goal," he once said. "My strength lies solely in my tenacity." Today we take for granted the fact that immunizations protect us from disease and that we can drink beverages without worry of food-poisoning, but the next time you enjoy a cold beverage, try and remember to thank Louis Pasteur's indefatigable persistence when it came to achieving his goals.

Consider Abraham Lincoln's persistence:

- In 1831, his business failed
- In 1832, he was defeated in his run for state legislator
- In 1833, another business attempt failed
- In 1835, his fiancee died
- In 1836, he had a nervous breakdown
- In 1843, he ran for Congress and was defeated
- In 1848, he was again defeated in his run for Congress
- In 1855, he ran for the Senate and was defeated
- In 1856, he ran for Vice President and lost
- In 1859, he ran for the Senate again and was defeated.
- In 1860, he was elected the 16th president of the United States.

Abraham Lincoln is a model of what can be achieved with persistence. With it, he shaped history; without it, we would not even know his name. The difference between our successes and failures will often be determined by our ability to persevere.

A high school football coach was attempting to motivate his players to persevere through a difficult stretch of close losses on the road. Halfway through the season, he stood before his team and said, "Did Michael Jordan ever quit?" The team responded, "No!" He yelled, "What about the Wright brothers? Did they ever give up?" "No!" the team resounded. "Did John Elway ever throw in the towel?" Again, the team yelled, "No!" "Did Elmer Williams ever quit?"

There was a long silence. Finally one player was bold enough to ask, "Who's Elmer Williams? We've never heard of him." The coach triumphantly snapped back, "Of course you never heard of him – he quit!"

Whatever our goals are, whether large goals such as becoming a professional athlete, inventing a new product, or starting a multimillion-dollar company, or smaller goals like shedding 15 pounds or getting out of credit card debt, our persistence toward obtaining that goal and our ability to "keep on keeping on" will determine our measure of success.

The two most important times of the day

"Each morning puts man on trial and each evening passes judgment."

–Roy L. Smith

Morning

"He who every morning has a plan for the transactions of the day and follows that plan carries thread that will guide him through the labyrinth of the most busy life."

-Victor Hugo

"Your morning thoughts may determine your conduct for the day."

–William M. Peck

Early morning is the most critical time of each day. How you spend the beginning of your day sets the stage for the remaining hours. *If you purposefully establish a routine for spending your early morning as you want to, you will have taken a giant step toward spending the rest of your life the way you want to.* How we spend our mornings is the litmus test for our degree of self-mastery. Do we wake up with a plan for the day or are we scrambling, wasting time figuring out what we must do? If we have a plan for the day, do we consistently follow it? Do we follow a purposefully predetermined, set routine which makes us more efficient and productive, and allows more time to think and relax? Or do we haphazardly scramble to get ready and out the door to make it to work just in time? *Our mornings expose the power of our routines. Whether our routines are made up of good habits or bad habits is most evident in how we spent our early morning hours.* If we are to get the most out of life and come closer to reaching our potential, it's crucial that we establish good habits that allow us to more effectively utilize our early morning hours.

Sluggards

"How long will you lie there, you sluggard? When will you get up from your sleep? A little sleep, a little slumber, a little folding of the hands to rest – and poverty will come on you like a bandit and scarcity like an armed man."

-Proverbs 6:9-11

"As a door turns on its hinges, so a sluggard turns on his bed."

-Proverbs 26:14

One reason that mornings are not productive and are commonly mad scrambles to get ready and out the door is because our mornings are too short. We simply don't schedule enough time to make them productive and keep them less stressful. We cherish our sleep in those early morning hours and wait as long as possible before dragging ourselves out of bed. There is a good reason for this pattern. Sleep deprivation is epidemic in this country. Our days are so busy and packed full of activity that we often sacrifice sufficient sleeping hours. Unfortunately this becomes a vicious cycle. With lack of sleep we have less energy and less focus throughout the day, and are therefore less efficient, needing more time to do the same tasks. So we work longer and harder, albeit less efficiently, and therefore require more sleep. Sleep deprivation also greatly reduces a person's chances of changing habits. As mentioned earlier, habits exist to conserve energy in thought and action. In addition, a great deal of effort is required for the conscious mind to retrain the subconscious. When we are mentally drained and physically exhausted, it is all the more difficult to override the subconscious and change the habit. So how to break this cycle of exhaustion, laziness, and inefficiency? The answer lies in the second most important time of the day – the evening hours.

Evening

"A man without a plan for the day is lost before he starts."

–Lewis K. Bendele

"Sum up at night what thou has done by day."

–Lord Herbert

The second most important part of each day is your evening. How you spend your evenings in part determines how you spend your early mornings. Mentally taking stock of what you accomplished during the day and planning out what to do the next day is important to get your morning started off right and give you a running start for the day ahead. Having a plan for the day and following through with that plan allows you to be more efficient and effective with your time. If every day you fail to accomplish something you wanted to accomplish, it's probably because you didn't plan it. As John Wooden put it, "Failing to plan is planning to fail." *You simply must plan and schedule the things you want to do each day or you simply won't do them.*

Take time now to think about, plan, and list possible morning and evening routines:

Morning Routine:

_____

_____

_____

_____

_____

_____

_____

_____

_____

_____

Evening Routine:

_____

_____

_____

_____

_____

_____

_____

_____

_____

_____

Tricks of the Trade
Techniques that work

"You can be anything you want to be in America today provided you have two things: a specific goal and a plan."

A.L. Williams

The Power of Goals

Set a goal

After identifying which habits you want to replace and understanding how changing a habit occurs, it's time to set goals for achieving habit change. The results of numerous studies leave no doubt that pcoplc who consistently set goals arc morc successful than people who don't. One such study, done by Damon Burton at the University of Idaho, found that not only are people who set goals significantly more successful than those who don't, the study also revealed that people who use goal-setting effectively also:

- Suffer less from stress and anxiety
- Concentrate better
- Demonstrate more self-confidence
- Are more efficient
- Consistently perform better

In fact, new research suggests that not only are people who set goals more successful than people who don't, they may also be happier.

Franklin Covey, a company widely known for its training courses for organizations and individuals, recently commissioned the Hase-Schannen Research organization to conduct a study on the power of setting goals and the reasons for success or failure in achieving those goals. Results of the study found a direct correlation between a person's satisfaction with life and the ability to successfully achieve goals. Those individuals who ranked their satisfaction with life as 8 or higher (on a 1 to 10 scale with 10 being very happy) were twice as likely to be people who set goals for themselves. "When you look at the results of the survey, it's not surprising to see that individuals who are happier with their lives tend to be the ones who are also successful at achieving their goals," said Stephen Covey, vice chairman of Franklin Covey.

Clearly, the ability to effectively set goals will help you change habits. But, you can increase your chances of successful habit change even more by having a plan.

Have a Plan and Stick to It

Results of the Hase-Schannen study also make it clear that having a plan greatly enhances an individual's chances of successfully achieving a goal. Those individuals who had a plan were 3½ times more likely to successfully achieve their goals than those individuals without a plan.

- 78 percent of successfully achieved goals had plans
- 22 percent of successfully achieved goals did not have plans

In addition to creating a plan, sticking to that original plan is an important element of success. According to the research, individuals who adhered to their original plan had a dramatically higher success rate than those who altered or changed their original plan. The study found that individuals who followed their original plans were more than five times more likely to achieve success than those who deviated from their original plan.

- 84 percent of goals were successfully achieved with the original plan
- 16 percent of goals were successfully achieved with a changed plan

Hyrum Smith, vice chairman of Franklin Covey, commenting on the results of the study said, "It's incredible what success can be achieved when a person incorporates a simple plan into their schedule."

Say it out loud

When we tell other people about our goals or intentions they become more real. We feel accountable for doing what we say. When our intentions are available for public consumption and public scrutiny, we feel a degree of accountability we might not otherwise feel. This may be why we are often reluctant to share our goals of habit change with other people. If we announce our intentions and fail, then other people will know about it, making the sting of failure that much worse. This is why telling other people about or intentions regarding habit change is such a powerful incentive to help us persevere and not give up.

Write it down and track your progress

There is extensive research showing that writing something down helps you stick to it.

Numerous studies demonstrate that when we write down our goals and ambitions we are far more likely to achieve them. This is because writing involves turning the abstract thoughts in our minds into concrete words on paper – a process that makes us crystallize exactly what our intentions are and how we will carry them out.

Like telling others about our intentions, writing them down makes them more real and we feel more accountability about following through. But writing down intentions has the added power of being more permanent. When we say something out loud, the words float on the air and then are gone. There is no lasting record or proof of what was said. When we write something down, however, it is much more permanent. There exist proof of our testimony that continually reminds us and holds us accountable for following through with our goals.

It's not only important to write down your goals, but also to track your progress towards those goals. According to the study by Hase-Schannen Research, the number one contributing factor, most common in all individuals successfully achieving their goals, was *reviewing progress towards those goals on a regular basis*. As Hyrum Smith points out, "While pursuing a goal involves a change of habit and, at times, lifestyle, establishing a way to track your success dramatically increases a person's chances for improvement."

Just how important is writing it down? A study was done on a Harvard graduating class. Thirty years after graduation, 80 percent of these graduates had no specific goals or ambitions, 15 percent had goals or ambitions that they only thought about, and 5 percent had written goals and ambitions (dreams with a specific plan of action). The 5 percent who wrote them down, not only surpassed the goals they had written for themselves (measured by assets) but, as a group, also had more net worth than the other 95 percent *combined*.

Good peer pressure and partners in crime

Another vital asset for those trying to change or establish habits is support from others. Family members, friends, and peers can provide support, encouragement, motivation, and serve as friendly reminders − all of which can make the difference between successfully implementing real change in your life, or continuing on with the status quo. When I decided to do a triathlon, my next-door neighbor happened to be training for one also, so we decided to train together. Not only did we help encourage, motivate, and remind each other of our goals, but we also felt obligated to reciprocate the same support we received. Even when I couldn't bear the thought of waking up at 5:00 A.M. to go swimming in cold water, I felt obligated to be there for my neighbor. I couldn't let him down. This added motivation often made the difference for me.

String on your finger.   Message on your mirror

Keeping the habit you would like to change or develop at the forefront of your mind is essential. As previously discussed, the key to habit change is getting your conscious mind to communicate with, train, and reprogram your subconscious. Habits are performed by our subconscious and will exist until our conscious mind finally gets our subconscious' attention and starts to train and reprogram it. This happens more quickly and easily the longer and more frequently the goal of our new habit is in our conscious thoughts.

I'm sure you're aware of the "string on your finger" technique for remembering something. Little mental cues like this really do help. As we discussed earlier, when we think about performing the desired habit, we activate the prefrontal cortex of the brain – the part of the brain responsible for taking action. Research has shown that by doing this, the brain actually "practices" performing the desired habit. Remember that the more we repeat a behavior, the more ingrained it becomes, even when the repetition takes place in our minds.

Try this: Write your desired habit on paper and tape it to the mirror above your sink. That way, every evening before you go to bed, and every morning while getting ready for the day, you will be reminded of your desired habit change. When reminded by the sign on your mirror, mentally perform the task. You will do this automatically to a certain extent, but any extra concentration on performing the task helps. By doing this simple step, you will perform the desired habit at least two extra times each day. This will quickly add up. Using the analogy of the plant from Chapter 2, the habit grows bigger and stronger, and the roots grow deeper, the more the habit is repeated. Soon the desired behavior will be a well-established habit with a very deep root system.

Another trick that helps make habit change easier is doing "pre-work." Let's say you want to develop the habit of running every morning, but it's a struggle to get out of bed and make yourself actually get outside and start. If you prepare the night before (do pre-work) it will help you avoid not following through with your planned early morning run. For instance, you can lay out your running clothes, running shoes, headphones, etc, right next to your bed the night before. That way, when the alarm goes off you have less to do to get ready for your run. The task seems a little less daunting, and there are fewer reasons (excuses) not to run. The more work you can do before your greatest moments of weakness (the times you are most susceptible to not following through), the less likely you are to skip performing the desired task.

Another benefit of this technique is that we mentally perform the task while we are doing the pre-work. Once again, this added repetition, even if just performed in our minds, helps the task become a habit.

Say It Out Loud

Take time now to make a list of family, friends, and colleagues to tell about your plan to change a habit:

_____

_____

_____

_____

_____

_____

_____

_____

_____

_____

Support Group / Partners in Crime

Take time now to make a list of family, friends, and colleagues who you will ask to support your plan to change a habit:

_____

_____

_____

_____

_____

Take time now to make a list of possible partners to help you with your habit change:

_____

_____

_____

_____

_____

Write It Down
(Tape this to bathroom mirror)

I _____ hereby proclaim that I

will commit myself to the following habit change this

_____ day of _____, _____.

Habit Change:

_____

_____

_____

_____

_____

_____

Signature _____ Date _____

Witness signature _____ Date _____

Jack D. Hodge

Is it possible? Do I have the potential?

Never underestimate human potential

Humans are amazing creatures with incredible potential, but too often this potential goes unrealized. For centuries, a commonly held belief was that it was impossible for a human being to run a mile in under four minutes. The belief was so strong and prevalent it came to be known as the four-minute *barrier*. Sports commentators said that it was inconceivable for an athlete to run a mile in under four minutes. The top athletes of the period understood that this was beyond human potential. Even physiologists believed running a sub-four-minute mile was well beyond the genetic limits of the human body and mind. It seems just about everyone accepted that a four-minute mile would be a barrier that no human would ever be capable of breaking –everyone, that is, except Roger Bannister.

> *"Fueled by my faith in my training, I will overcome all obstacles."*
>
> *-Roger Bannister*

On May 6, 1954, Bannister became the first human to do the impossible – run a mile in under four minutes. That race is still referred to as the "Miracle Mile." But, the most important part of this story is often left out. Although it was widely believed to be impossible for a human to run a sub-four-mile, and although this barrier stood unchallenged for so long, Roger Bannister finally broke the "barrier," and in doing so, he unleashed human potential. By doing the impossible, he made everyone else realize that, if it could be done once, it could be done again. In fact, after breaking a barrier that stood for so long, Bannister's record only stood for 46 days before being broken again, then again, and again by others. Now hundreds of runners consistently break the four-minute "barrier," including several high school students every year. Once the athletes were liberated from this self-imposed limitation, the power of human potential was unleashed.

Never underestimate your potential

We all have vast resources of potential just waiting for us to tap into. The problem is that we often don't really believe the potential is there. The following story illustrates this point.

One night, a man in a bar had too much to drink. Instead of risking the drive home while intoxicated, he decided to walk. On his way home, it started storming, so the man decided to take a short-cut home through a graveyard to get out of the weather. Unfortunately because the night was dark and rainy, the man did not see an empty, freshly dug grave, and he fell in. He tried and tried to climb out of the hole but because the rain had made the sides of the hole so muddy and slippery, and because of the man's intoxicated state, he could not escape the grave. Exhausted and drunk, he curled up into a ball in the corner of the dark hole and fell asleep.

It just so happened that another man with the same plight was taking a short cut through the same graveyard. He too failed to see the grave and fell in. After trying with every last bit of his energy, he too finally conceded that there was no way he was getting out of the grave that night. During all the commotion, the first man woke up. Hidden from sight in the dark corner of the hole, in a deep, raspy voice, he said, "You will never get out of here." Hearing the gravelly voice from the dark corner of what the second man thought was an empty grave, the second man leaped out of the hole in one swift motion and ran all the way home without slowing down.

The point of the story is that although the second man truly believed he could not get out of the grave, he unknowingly possessed the potential to do so. Too often, we are just like this man. We greatly underestimate our own potential.

"As is" vs. "What can be"

Beware of shortchanging your potential by accepting the world "as is" rather than exploring the possibilities and applying your energies to "what can be." The following story by Mark Twain illustrates how people often don't live up to their potential.

A man dies and meets Saint Peter at the pearly gates. Realizing Saint Peter was a wise and knowledgeable fellow, he said, "Saint Peter, I have been interested in military history for many years. Tell me, who was the greatest general of all time?"

Saint Peter quickly responded, "Oh, that is a simple question. It's that man right over there," as he pointed nearby.

The man said, "You must be mistaken, Saint Peter. I knew that man on Earth and he was just a common laborer."

"That's right, my friend," replied Saint Peter. "But he would have been the greatest general of all time...if he had been a general."

We all can do much more than we think is possible. Don't sell yourself short.

Today vs. Tomorrow
Dreamers and Doers

**Tomorrow is the most powerful
weapon of the dreamer.
Today is the most powerful
weapon of the doer.**

"Tomorrow is the day when idlers work, and fools reform, and mortal men lay hold of heaven."

-Edward Young.

If you have any ambitions of becoming a doer, you must start today. There is only today. You cannot rely on starting tomorrow. *If tomorrow is in your resolution, tomorrow will be your dissolution.* If you plan to start tomorrow, you have no chance of becoming a doer. You are merely fooling yourself. Famed author Marie Edgeworth understood the importance of starting resolutions today instead of tomorrow. She wrote: "The man who will not execute his resolutions today when they are fresh upon him can have no hope from them tomorrow; they will be dissipated, lost and perish in the hurry and scurry of the world, or sunk in the slough of indolence." When Nolan Bushell, the founder of Atari, was asked about his entrepreneurial success, he responded, "The critical ingredient is getting off your tush and doing something. It's as simple as that. A lot of people have ideas, but there are few who decide to do something about them now. Not tomorrow. Not next week, but today. The true entrepreneur is a doer, not a dreamer."

This transformation from dreamer to doer is not painless; it comes only with great effort. But it is achievable – I'm living proof. There was no bigger dreamer than me. Lack of self-mastery was my disease. Inaction, procrastination, lack of commitment, and lack of resolve were the symptoms. My self-treatment was the word "tomorrow." The use of the word tomorrow in my resolve always soothed my symptoms for a time, but they always came back needing yet another fix of "tomorrow." I was treating the symptoms, when what I needed was a treatment for my disease (lack of self-mastery). That's exactly what "doing something you hate every day just for practice" was for me, and that's exactly what it will be for you too – regardless of your level of self-mastery now. But this practiced discipline must start today.

The Someday Syndrome

Someday Syndrome

"Someday when I grow up, finish school and get a job, I'll start living my life the way I want...Someday after the mortgage is paid off, the finances are on track and the kids are grown up, I'll drive that new car and take exciting trips abroad...Someday, now that I'm about to retire, I'll buy that beautiful motor home and travel across this great country, and see all there is to see...someday."

-Ed Foreman

Too often, we believe there is some far better future out there just waiting to spring itself upon our lives. Somehow, someway, someday it will just happen. This wishful thinking is not based in reality, but is pervasive non-the-less.

Somehow, someway, someday:

I'll get that job of my dreams
I'll start exercising
I'll start eating healthy
I'll get out of debt
I'll get on a budget
I'll get that promotion
I'll start volunteering my time
My marriage will transform itself
I'll start spending more time with the kids...

Somehow, someway, someday it will just happen.

Call to Action

As mentioned earlier, the difference between the dreamer and the doer is consistent, purposeful action. Action is the quintessential prerequisite for any change to occur. Too often we talk about, think about, dream about, hope for, even plan on doing extraordinary things without any execution or follow-through on our part. If we are to experience real, purposeful change, we must take real, purposeful action. This is essential to intentional living. As my grandfather often said – "what's the difference between good deeds and good intentions? Everything!" Cavett Robert, one of the nation's outstanding public speakers, wrote, "A constructive life is built of the things we do – not of the things we don't do. Never forget that the only material which can be used in building a life is positive action."

Suppose there were five birds perched in a tree. Now suppose three of the birds decided to fly away. How many birds would be left in the tree?

Five birds would remain in the tree. Making the decision to fly away and actually flying away are two very different things. The difference is action.

"The one thing that separates winners from losers is, winners take action!

-Anthony Robbins

"Action, action, and still more action."

-Theodore Roosevelt

The point of this analogy may seem simplistic and obvious, but its wisdom is often ignored. Too many people wait for change to occur, expecting they will somehow, someway, someday wake up and be the person they've dreamed of being. This is clearly foolishness, but every dreamer is guilty of such delusions. The doers, on the other hand, take action and make change occur.

During the Great Depression, in 1932, a young man graduated from college with a degree in social science. He had no direction and no idea of what he wanted to do with his life. Compounding his predicament was the fact that jobs were very scarce at the time. The young man decided to wait for good fortune to befall him. In the meantime, during the summer, he went back to his old lifeguarding job at a local swimming pool to earn some money.

A father of some of the children at the pool befriended the young man and took an interest in his future. He encouraged the young man to look inside himself and decide what he most wanted to do. Acting on this advice, the young lifeguard spent the next several days searching his heart. Finally, he knew what he wanted to do. He made the decision to become a radio announcer.

The young man shared his dream of becoming a radio announcer with his mentor who told him to begin taking the necessary action to make his dream come true. The young man set out hitchhiking through Illinois and Iowa, determined to break into the radio business. Eventually he landed a job in Davenport, Iowa, working for WKOC as a sports announcer.

"Finally finding a job was nice" the man would later admit, "but what I learned about taking action was infinitely more valuable." This experience was the first of many that required former President Ronald Reagan to combine a dream with determined, purposeful action.

What ideas, dreams, or good intentions have you allowed to sit idly perched in a tree because your decision wasn't backed by purposeful action?

Lillian Katz understood that fortune wasn't looking for her; she would have to take action and hunt fortune down. As a 24-year-old, pregnant with her first child, Lillian sought a way to increase her family's meager income. Using $2,000 saved from wedding gifts, she purchased a few supplies and submitted an ad to a popular magazine promoting personalized handbags and belts. The year was 1951, and at the time, the thought of putting a person's initials on products was novel and somewhat revolutionary. The ad read: "Be the first to sport that personalized look."

The orders starting coming in, business grew, and today her mail-order catalog company, Lillian Vernon Corporation, enjoys annual sales of nearly $200 million. No longer does Lillian fill orders at her kitchen table. Her company now employs more than1,000 people to process more than 30,000 weekly orders. This success was not a result of Lillian waiting around for her family income to increase. She took purposeful action and made it happen.

Successful people make the most of their circumstances and seize any opportunities that come their way. The following story tells of a man who did just the opposite.

A great flood threatened a man's home. As the water rose to the man's front porch, a neighbor in a four-wheel-drive truck offered the man a ride to escape to safety. The man refused, explaining that he had faith that God would save him. As the floodwaters continued to rise, the man eventually had to retreat to the roof of his house.

At this point, a man in a boat came by and offered the stranded man a ride to safety. The man again declined the offer, explaining that he had faith that God would save him.

As the water level reached the top of the man's roof and it looked as though he would not survive, a helicopter flew down and dropped a rope to rescue the man from certain drowning. Once more the man declined to be rescued and refused to take hold of the rope explaining that he had faith that God would save him. Now, stranded at the highest point of the roof and facing certain death, the man called out to God: "God, I had faith that you would save me. Why have you not done so?"

Suddenly a voice boomed from the heavens as God exclaimed: "What do you want from me? I sent you a truck, a boat, and even a helicopter!"

Living intentionally takes action on our part. We've all been equipped with the tools, abilities, and circumstances necessary to reach our God-given potential. But reaching that potential requires action – consistent, purposeful action. So, what are you waiting for? Take action today! Set your course and utilize the power of habit!

BIBLIOGRAPHY

Abbott, Lawrence. 1920. *Impressions of Theodore Roosevelt*. Garden City (New York): Doubleday, Page.

Alford, Steve. 1989. *Playing for Knight: my six seasons with Coach Knight.* New York. Simon & Schuster.

Amos, James E. 1927. *Theodore Roosevelt: Hero to His Valet*. New York: John Day.

Axelrod, Alan. 1999. *Patton on Leadership*. New Jersey: Prentice Hall Press.

Basler, Roy P. 1946. *Abraham Lincoln: His Speeches and Writings*. New York: World Publishing Co.

Basler, Roy P. 1953. *The Collected Works of Abraham Lincoln.* 8 vols. New Brunswick (New Jersey): Rutgers Univ. Press.

Beveridge, Albert J. 1928. *Abraham Lincoln: 1809-1858*. 4 vols. New York: Houghton Mifflin.

Bishop, Joseph Bucklin. 1920. *Theodore Roosevelt and His Time – Shown in His Own Letters.* 2 vols. New York: Charles Scribner's Sons.

Blum, John Morton. 1993. *The Republican Roosevelt.* 2nd ed. Cambridge (Massachusetts): Harvard University Press.

Bryce, James. 1995 reprint [1888]. *The American Commonwealth.* 2 vols. Indianapolis (Indiana): Liberty Fund.

Chambers, Oswald. 1963. *My Utmost for His Highest.* Uhrichsville, Ohio: Barbour.

Charnwood, Lord. 1924. *Theodore Roosevelt.* Boston: Atlantic Monthly Press.

Cohen, William A. 2001. *Wisdom of the Generals.* New Jersey: Prentice Hall Press.

Collins, Jim. 2001. *Good to Great.* New York: Harper Collins.

Cook, John. 1993. *The Book of Positive Quotations.* New York: Gramercy Books.

Crocker, H. W., III. 1999. *Robert E. Lee on Leadership.* Rocklin (California): Prima.

Einstein, Lewis. 1930. *Roosevelt: His Mind in Action.* Cambridge (Massachusetts): Riverside.

Eldredge, John. 2001. *Wild at Heart.* Nashville: Thomas Nelson Publishers.

Frank, Leonard Roy. 2001. *Quotationary*. New York: Random House.

Freedman, David H. 2000. *Corps Business: The 30 Management Principles of the U.S. Marines.* New York: Harper Collins.

Gable, John Allen. 1978. *The Bull Moose Years.* Port Washington (New York): Kennikart Press.

Gladwell, Malcolm. 2000. The Tipping Point: *How Little Things Can Make a Big Difference.* New York: Back Bay Books.

Hagedorn, Hermann. 1950 reprint [1919]. *The Boy's Life of Theodore Roosevelt.* New York: Harper & Brothers.

Harbaugh, William H. 1997 reprint [1961]. Pow*er and Responsibility: The Life and Times of Theodore Roosevelt.* Newton (Connecticut): American Political Biography Press.

Henderson, Daniel. 1919. *"Great-Heart" – The Life Story of Theodore Roosevelt.* 2nd ed. New York: William Edwin Rudge.

Hunter, James C. 1998. *Servant Leadership.* Rocklin (California): Prima.

Jamison, Steve. 1997. *Wooden.* Chicago: Contemporary Books.

Johnston, William Davison. 1981 reprint [1958]. *TR: Champion of the Strenous Life*. New York: Theodore Roosevelt Association.

Maxwell, John C. 1999. *The Twenty-one Indispensable Qualities of a Leader*. Nashville: Thomas Nelson Publishers.

Maxwell, John C. 1999. *The Twenty-one Irrefutable Laws of Leadership*. Nashville: Thomas Nelson Publishers.

Maxwell, John C. 2000. *The Twenty-one Most Powerful Minutes in a Leaders Day*. Nashville: Thomas Nelson Publishers.

McCormick, Blaine. 2001. *At Work with Thomas Edison: Ten Business Lessons from America's Greatest Innovator*. New York: Entrepreneur Press.

Naylor, Natalie A., Douglas Brinkley, and John Allen Gable (eds.). 1992. *Theodore Roosevelt: Many-Sided American*. Interlaken (New York): Heart of the Lakes Publishing.

Neff, Thomas J., Citrin, James M. 2002. *Lessons from the Top: The 50 Most Successful Business Leaders in America – and What You Can Learn from Them*. New York: Currency Doubleday.

Roosevelt, Theodore. 1995. *A Bully Father: Theodore Roosevelt's Letters to His Children*. Kerr, Joan Paterson (ed.). New York: Random House.

Simonton, Dean Keith. 1994. *Greatness: Who Makes History and Why.* New York: Guilford Press.

Strock, James M. 2001.*Theodore Roosevelt on Leadership.* Roseville (California): Prima.

Strouse, Jean. 2000. *Morgan: American Financier.* New York: Perennial.
Taylor, Robert L. 1996. Milita*ry Leadership: In Pursuit of Excellence.* Boulder (Colorado): Westview Press.

Warren, Rick. 2002. *The Purpose Driven Life.* Grand Rapids, Michigan: Zondervan.

Williams, T. Harry. 1952. *Lincoln and His Generals.* New York: Alfred A. Knopf.

Made in the USA
Lexington, KY
12 April 2012